GLOUCESTER MASSACHUSETTS

QUARRY BOOKS

The Stress~Free Home

Beautiful Interiors for Serenity and Harmonious Living

Jackie Craven

First paperback published in the United States of America by
Quarry Books, an imprint of
Rockport Publishers, Inc.
33 Commercial Street
Gloucester, Massachusetts 01930-5089
Telephone: (978) 282-9590
Fax: (978) 283-2742
www.rockpub.com

Library of Congress Cataloging-in-Publication Data available

ISBN 1-59253-138-5

10 9 8 7 6 5 4 3 2 1

Design: Yee Design
Cover/Spine Image: Eric Roth
Back Cover Images: Courtesy of Zimmer + Rohoe, left and middle; Courtesty of R.O.O.M., right

Printed in China

Acknowledgments

The spirit of home and the comfort we find there is at the heart of any book on interior design. The talented designers and photographers whose work is reflected here capture that spirit, and I am deeply grateful.

For shepherding this project from inspiration to completion, I thank the entire team at Rockport Publishers, most especially Betsy Gammons, who never failed to find just the right photograph and to speak just the right words of encouragement. I am grateful to my agent, Barbara Doyen, for introducing us.

For twenty-five years of unwavering friendship and support, I thank all the members of my writer's group: Pauline Bartel, Joyce Bouyea, David Lee Drotar, Kate Kunz, Jane Streiff, and Donna Tomb.

Finally, my deepest appreciation goes to Susan Carroll Jewell, whose probing questions and original thought helped shape the direction of this book. Because of her professional research, invaluable writing, and eagle-eyed editing, the sometimes stressful job of working with words was for me a more wondrous and serene experience.

Contents

Chapter One

Patterns for Peaceful Living

**"This is the true nature of home—it is the place of Peace;
the shelter, not only from injury, but from all terror, doubt and division."**

John Ruskin (1819–1900), English author and art critic

Imagine a moment when you felt completely at peace. Perhaps you were strolling by a lake, kneeling in a temple, or relaxing on the porch of your childhood home. There were no ringing telephones, no petty quarrels, no pressing deadlines, no terrifying news reports. Worries slipped away and you seemed to merge with the flicker of light and shadow, the song of a bird, or the scent of lilacs. ▪ Sensations like these are all too fleeting. In a world of technological wonders, we are surrounded by uncertainties. We may be haunted by past events or anxious about what lies ahead. In the hectic pace of our lives, we often overlook the things that can bring us peace: the rhythm of falling rain, the bewitching interplay of color and pattern, the simple joys of kneading bread, stoking a fire, or rocking in a comfortable chair. ▪ A home designed for stress-free living evokes this type of serenity. Comfortable and convenient, beautiful and uncomplicated, it nurtures body, mind, and spirit. The design may begin with choosing restful colors, patterns, and shapes, yet these elements alone won't make a home tranquil. Creating peaceful, soothing environments involves the orchestration of many components, from the material details of fabrics and furnishings to the ethereal energies that all things possess. ▪ By combining these elements in ways that calm and delight, the stress-free home encourages love, camaraderie, and spiritual connectedness.

serenity secret #1

Wrap yourself in softness. A cozy chenille throw, savored for its color and texture, can become your serenity blanket, recalling the comfort and safety you felt as a child. Save your serenity blanket for times when you especially need warmth and reassurance.

opposite *Serene spaces do not need to be minimalist or monochrome. Flowing draperies and carefully balanced colors bring a sense of tranquility to a cozy seating area.*

Designing for Serenity: two approaches

the Zen home	the stress-free home
Open spaces	Private spaces
White or neutral walls	Healing colors
Streamlined, functional furnishings	Ergonomic furnishings
Balanced, symmetrical arrangements	Soothing shapes and patterns
Natural fabrics and finishings	Eco-friendly materials
Minimal decorations	Carefully selected artifacts

opposite *The most restful bedrooms are uncomplicated. A firm mattress, pure cotton linens, and plenty of fresh air are all that's needed for a sound sleep.*

The Quest for Peace

Common sense tells us that every home should be relaxing and stress-free. Our homes are, after all, our shelter, our refuge, and the expression of our personalities and creativity. But, somewhere along the way, the ideal of home has become distorted. It's so easy to be swept away by fashion trends and enticing store window displays. Like tourists who have boarded the wrong bus, we may discover ourselves in a very different kind of home than the one we really need. We acquire chairs that cause backaches, collections that require dusting and polishing, carpeting that emits toxic fumes, entertainment centers that command our attention, electronics that click and beep and rattle our nerves, and books and papers that grow into weary piles of obligation. We spend countless hours cleaning and maintaining possessions that bring little joy, and everywhere we look, we are reminded of our frustrations and losses.

The quest for stress-free living has inspired a simpler, more orderly approach to decorating. Many designers have turned to the clean, uncluttered style drawn from the teachings of Zen Buddhism. In its most pure form, Zen design seeks escape from worldly worries. Furniture is selected for functionality and arranged with an eye toward symmetry and balance. Muted colors and expansive spaces encourage the tranquil state of self-forgetfulness. Earth-inspired patterns and textures, applied with restraint, express an appreciation for nature.

However, your home need not be monotone or minimalist to evoke a peaceful atmosphere. For many of us, peace comes not through self-forgetting but through self-remembering. You may feel more relaxed and more centered when you surround yourself with objects that express your cultural heritage. The desire for warm, comforting spaces may mean introducing plush cushions, a bright splash of color, and carefully chosen artifacts. The iron skillet Grandmother once used, the finger painting made by a child who is now grown, and a storybook from your own childhood provide important connections with the past and the future. While avoiding excess, truly peaceful environments remind us where we have been and where we are going.

right A stress-free home will allow you to express your creativity and affirm cultural connections. The design is orderly and clutter-free, yet rich in details that have personal meaning. Here, a handcrafted footstool and woven carpets bring warmth and meaning to a symmetrical arrangement of matching chairs.

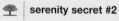 serenity secret #2

Take comfort in a talisman. The ancients used crystals and amulets, but you need not believe in magic to feel the calming effect of a cherished object. Let a treasured heirloom or a favorite work of art serve as your symbol of safety and protection, bringing reassurance during times of stress.

Coping with Stress

As you plan your living space, your first step is to identify those things that sap your serenity and cause discord in your household. Sources of stress are all around us. Harsh music blaring from the house next door and pressures from an employer will easily arouse tensions and anxiety. A fluctuating stock market and news of terrorism or war can create an overwhelming sense of foreboding. Even a joyous event such as the birth of a child or an important career advance will stir up a tidal wave of emotions. Big events and minor nuisances, devastating losses and sudden successes will all lead to tightened muscles, rapid heartbeat, and other physiological symptoms we associate with stress.

All too frequently the things that distress us are circumstances we cannot control. We can, however, design living spaces that will help us cope with random world events, ease family conflicts, and calm the inner demons that kindle fear and discontent.

Make Easy Changes

Minimizing the impact of stressful events begins with identifying things you have control over and taking small, simple actions. Although you may not be able to alter political events, you can monitor how often you listen to the news. A chronic health problem may be beyond your control, but you still have the power to fill your home with soothing herbal fragrances. Sometimes even an unrelated action such as painting a door will bring a fresh outlook and open the way to new beginnings. Simply rearranging the furniture is healing, allowing you to shape your environment in meaningful ways.

Move Slowly

Changing the appearance or layout of your home is, in itself, potentially stressful. Instead of throwing the entire household into upheaval, work on one room or even a single corner. Instead of emptying a closet, clean out a single drawer. Be cautious about removing photographs and mementos. Memories that are painful to you now may be treasured years later. For an easier transition, remove sentimental items gradually and keep them in storage.

"I too am a rare
Pattern... As I wander down
The garden-paths."

Amy Lowell (1874–1925), American poet

🌳 serenity secret #3

Eat a strawberry, a peach, or a slice of melon. Close your eyes and chew slowly, savoring the flavor and texture. Focusing on sensual details is one way to clear the mind and relieve anxieties. To enhance your pleasure, prepare a bowl of mixed fruit and try to identify each flavor—without peeking.

Work from the Inside Out

The atmosphere of a room is more than the sum of its decor. Things we cannot explain or even name will exert subtle influence on your emotional state. To create spaces where you will feel at peace, listen closely to your instincts and choose details that resonate for you. Consider all the senses: sight, sound, scent, touch, and taste. Also, do not forget subtle environmental influences such as temperature, humidity, lighting, and ventilation.

Involve the Entire Family

Designing for serenity is a personal process, but it affects much more than the self. Through the harmonious arrangement of colors, patterns, and shapes we hope to encourage harmony in our relationships. Every being in the household—children, pets, and aging parents—will be impacted by seemingly insignificant details in the environment. Designing living areas and other shared spaces will call for friendly negotiations and carefully considered compromises. One person's passion for plush cushions may yield to another's appreciation for sleek metallics, while fabrics and wallcoverings may incorporate the favorite colors of several family members.

Design Guidelines

There are no rigid rules for designing a stress-free environment. We each draw comfort and strength from different sources. The answers for you may lie in ancient Eastern philosophies or in classical principles of design. You may be intrigued by the findings of modern psychologists only to return, once again, to lessons you learned from your grandmother. Creating a stress-free home is a journey of exploration and self-discovery. Use these guidelines as a starting point for creating spaces that bring you tranquility.

Floor Plans

The most serene environments acknowledge fundamental human needs for space and privacy. Designing a stress-free home may mean rethinking the placement of rooms and furnishings. Expansive, open areas will evoke a sense of freedom, but cozy, comforting nooks are often preferred for relaxation and meditation. Comfort and convenience are key when planning rooms. Modern theories of ergonomics encourage stress-free living

above *Natural sunlight, earth-inspired colors, and bowls of fresh fruit make the kitchen a pleasing area to celebrate simple comforts.*

"Reduce big troubles to small ones, and small ones to nothing."

Chinese proverb

Tranquility Tools

Vástu Shástra:
Follow guidelines from ancient India for harmonious floor plans and furniture arrangements.

Feng Shui:
Balance the flow of energies according to ancient Chinese philosophies.

Celestial Design:
Look to the stars and find inspiration in early tribal customs.

Spiritual Geometry:
Seek archetypal shapes and patterns that express a sense of universal order.

Hydrotherapy:
Celebrate the healing power of water in home spas and other indoor waterspaces.

Aromatherapy:
Use healing aromas from fresh flowers, dried herbs, and essential oils.

Color Therapy:
Choose colors for their proven ability to affect emotions and physical well-being.

Light Therapy:
Flood rooms with the healing rays of full-spectrum lighting.

Air and Water Purifiers:
Free the home from stress-inducing pollutants.

Sound Conditioners:
Mask distracting outside noise with soothing music and sounds drawn from nature.

Gestalt Psychology:
Explore the deeper emotional contexts of rooms and their decor.

Jungian Analysis:
Make meaningful symbols the focal point for your rooms.

through easy-reach storage, step-saving furniture arrangements, and seating that promotes healthy posture. Many designers also look to *feng shui, vástu shástra,* and other ancient philosophies for ideas on ways to redirect the flow of energy through the home.

Shapes and Lines

Every room is unique, expressing the personalities and values of those who live there. Nevertheless, we all have a seemingly inborn need for what is often called the "universal principles of design." Our sense of unity, proportion, and balance will often determine whether a room feels "right." An undersized painting on a long, blank wall can create an undercurrent of unrest. A single, heavy armoire at the far end of a room can make the space feel lopsided, upsetting our equilibrium. However, the need for balance and order does not mean that our homes must be perfectly symmetrical. Instead, you are likely to discover a great deal of quiet excitement in the subtle interplay of line, shape, form, and pattern. An inviting grouping of chairs or an exquisite collection of pottery can provide a satisfying counterpoint to other items in the room.

Sensual Details

Numerous studies have shown that color and light will trigger strong physiological and emotional responses. Peaceful rooms make full use of mood-enhancing light from the Sun or from specially designed full-spectrum fixtures. Healing colors, noted for their calming effects, are drawn from earth, sea, and sky. Other sensual details, selected for their soothing properties and medicinal powers, add richness and texture to the atmosphere. The gentle notes of a wind chime, the restful scent of lavender, and, perhaps, even the energizing taste of strawberries become as important to the room as its furnishings.

Physical Health

A peaceful mind begins with a healthy body; a serene living space will nurture and protect the physical well-being of all who enter. Natural fabrics and finishes are preferred not only because they are beautiful but also because they are free of formaldehyde and other toxic chemicals. Uncomplicated and comforting bedcovers are made from unbleached, untreated cotton. Plush woolen area rugs or grassy sisal floor mats replace synthetic wall-to-wall carpeting. Warm, natural sunlight and lush aromas become an important part of the design because they please the senses and also have a proven power to heal.

Nature and Technology

No home is an island. It must exist in a larger environment and it must utilize natural resources. A peaceful dwelling is eco-friendly. The use of biodegradable and recycled materials expresses a reverence for nature. Flourishing plant life and indoor fountains reflect spiritual ties with the natural world. Appliances are selected for their compact shapes and their energy efficiency. Computers, televisions, and other electronics are incorporated in pleasing, unobtrusive ways.

Artifacts

There is no question that clutter rattles our nerves and drains our spirits. As you re-create your home, you and your family will want to seek ways to clear away or sensibly store papers, books, and odd assortments of knick-knacks. Designing tranquil spaces is a process of deciding what is important and what is not. Consequently, home design becomes a deep and gradual process of self-analysis. Art and artifacts that have personal meaning or symbolic significance become key elements in the design of a home that is truly serene.

As You Begin . . .

Serenity is expressed through things we can see—colors, patterns, and shapes—but it is also sensed through the heart. A stress-free home encourages inner calm and spiritual enlightenment. It fosters peaceful relations between life partners, reaffirms connections with nature, and expresses caring and respect for the environment.

Take inspiration from the serene rooms photographed here and pause for quiet reflection. Think about favorite places from your past and beautiful rooms you've only imagined. Write down your dreams, or draw pictures and floor plans for the home you would like to create. As you begin to make small changes, notice how the atmosphere shifts. Talk with family and friends, and decide which strategies work best for you. Serenity does not come with a flash or a boom but with a gradual warming of the spirit. Let it begin now.

 serenity secret #4

Paint your bathroom blue. Pale, watery colors vibrate at frequencies you'll find naturally soothing. For deep relaxation, sprinkle your bathwater with lavender oil and bathe in the silvery blue hue of moonlight.

opposite *Tucked in a narrow alcove, a tranquil bathing area evokes the atmosphere of sky and sea. The hand spray allows for soothing hydromassage.*

Chapter Two

Ancient Wisdoms

All things in the universe are composed of energy; endlessly rotating electrons and neutrons make up every living thing, every object, every swirling gas and grain of dust. Modern physicists are only just beginning to unlock the mysteries of energy and matter, but philosophers have been exploring these concepts since before the dawn of recorded history. In some cultures, ruminations about the forces of nature have evolved into sophisticated guidelines for aligning energies and achieving order and balance in our lives. ▪

Perhaps the best-known philosophies are *feng shui,* originating in China, and *vástu shástra,* originating in India. Both philosophies teach that electrical, magnetic, and gravitational forces influence every aspect of human activity. For the uninitiated, the theories may seem strange and incomprehensible, yet both *feng shui* and *vástu shástra* offer specific, practical advice for the placement of rooms, furnishings, and decorative details. Their teachings suggest reasons why some rooms feel cold and uninviting while others lift our spirits, why the baby wakes in the night, and why the cat tears through the house as though its tail was on fire. Moreover, these philosophies offer solutions—often minor adjustments in room decoration—to resolve conflicts and restore harmony.

 serenity secret #5

Check your *chi*. Frequent quarrels or emotional upsets could be due to an excess of *yang* energy in the passionate southern portion of your home, say *feng shui* pratitioners. Place a large clay pot filled with yellow primroses in that area. The *yin* energy of the earthen clay and the flowers will help stabilize the energies and encourage family harmony. At the very least, they'll cheer you up.

opposite *Ancient Chinese warriors used reflective armor to deflect hostile energies and protect themselves from harm. Modern* feng shui *practitioners often use mirrors to channel energies through the home. To avoid "beheading" viewers, choose mirrors that are very tall.*

"The most beautiful thing we can experience is the mysterious."

Albert Einstein (1879–1955), German-born U.S. physicist

Dual Energies

yin design	yang design
To create stress-free rooms, choose shapes, colors, and textures that contain tranquil *yin* energy.	For home offices, kitchens, and other high-activity areas, choose shapes, colors, and textures that contain stimulating *yang* energy.
Thin, wavy lines	Straight or angular lines
Blue, green, and pastel colors	Red and orange
Soft carpeting	Glass, marble, and stone
Flowing drapery	Wooden or metal window blinds
Cushioned furniture	Unupholstered furnishings

opposite *According to feng shui beliefs, the curved shape and padded cushions give this chair a quiet yin quality, making it conducive for relaxation and meditation. The red pillow, however, is yang, which suggests fire energy and promotes fame and power. Together, these yin yang forces invite both alertness and concentration.*

Feng shui and *vástu shástra* date back thousands of years, but, even before these systems were developed, prehistoric peoples observed the heavens and theorized that mystical life energies, controlled by the movement of the Sun, Moon, and stars, shaped the happiness and well-being of every individual. In all parts of the world, tribes have developed rituals and symbols to help members harmonize with natural forces and thereby improve their emotional and psychological well-being.

Today, few of us remember our ties to the earth; we are often unaware of planetary movements and we do not consider the powerful energies that all things possess. Our spirits may resemble wildly swinging pendulums, unable to find the quiet still point at the center. Revisiting ancient and prehistoric beliefs is one way to reconnect with natural forces and to rediscover the things that bring us the greatest level of peace and joy.

Feng Shui

Feng shui is not one philosophy but many. The complex system of ideas began in China and spread through Tibet and the rest of Asia. Over the course of six thousand years, the tools and techniques expanded to include a broad range of ideas and approaches. At its most basic level, *feng shui* (meaning *wind/water*) offers ways to channel life energies (called *chi*). According to *feng shui* teachings, all things in the universe are made up of two polar energies, *yin* and *yang*. A profoundly restful environment has more *yin* energy: every aspect of the decor encourages peace or introspection. A room that excites and inspires is predominantly *yang:* the decor promotes activity and extroversion. However, both *yin* and *yang* are essential to life, and the goal of *feng shui* is to achieve a harmonious balance between the two.

**"Just remain in the center, watching.
And then forget that you are there."**

Lau-Tzu (604–531 B.C.), Chinese spiritual leader

To achieve this, some practitioners look closely at surrounding geographic features such as mountains, streams, buildings, and roads. Others use a compass to determine the most favorable directions according to precise mathematical calculations. Today, many *feng shui* followers take an eclectic approach, combining the ancient laws with color healing, astrology, and an assortment of modern tools such as air ionizers and electromagnetic radiation detectors.

Regardless of the approach used, designing your home according to *feng shui* principles means paying close attention to the flow of *chi* through its rooms and fine-tuning your instincts for what "feels right." You may want to seek advice from a trained *feng shui* practitioner (a *geomancer*), or you may choose to merely sample the ancient Chinese art. Even minor changes made according to *feng shui* guidelines can make a dramatic difference in the atmosphere your home evokes.

Feng Shui Tips

- *Consult a ba-gua chart to find the most favorable energy centers.*
- *Clear away clutter, meaningless collections, and unused furnishings.*
- *Seek balance in furniture arrangements.*
- *Use lighting, mirrors, crystals, and chimes to direct the flow of energy.*
- *Use plants to soften sharp, jutting angles and to energize stagnant corners.*
- *Make sure all doors and windows open easily, even if you never use them.*
- *Choose natural materials for fabrics, furnishings, floors, and countertops.*
- *Repair leaking faucets promptly.*
- *Make sure water in flower vases, fountains, and fish tanks is fresh.*

Ba-gua Basics

In this simplified version of the ba-gua, no compass is required. Simply align the bottom of the chart with your front door. Then, observe where the energy centers fall in relationship to the rooms in your home.

wealth and prosperity	fame and success	love and marriage
family	wholeness and health	children and creativity
learning and knowledge	career	helpful people

opposite *Modern design mingles with ancient wisdoms in this sleek, efficient kitchen. The sink is placed away from the stove, assuring harmony between fire and water elements. Smooth, rounded work surfaces invite a smooth flow of energy.*

below *Cherished by the ancients, sunlight, water, and blooming foliage combine to create a deeply soothing bathing area.*

The *Ba-gua*

A helpful tool used by many *feng shui* believers is the *ba-gua*. This eight-sided diagram is derived from the *I-Ching,* the Chinese book of Divination, and serves as an energy map for your home. Each side of the diagram represents a different aspect of life and suggests the most favorable locations for important daily activities. There are many variations of the *ba-gua;* some specify compass directions while others simply show where your home's energy centers fall in relation to your front door. Regardless of the method used, the goal is to identify the areas in your home where energies are strong, and areas that need "energy adjustments." Once you have this knowledge, you can employ a variety of *feng shui* cures.

Vástu Shástra

When you explore *vástu shástra,* you move even farther back in time than *feng shui.* Thousands of years ago, before *feng shui* evolved in China, Hindus in India taught that our dwellings should exist in harmony with nature and the universe. The sacred Hindu scriptures, the *Vedas,* set forth a series of design principles known as *vástu shástra,* also called *sthapatya ved,* or *Vedic* design. Drawing upon *jyotish* (Indian astrology), the principles describe the planetary forces on the natural elements and, consequently, on worldly circumstances. Creating a stress-free environment means aligning those forces so that the dweller, the dwelling, and the cosmos are in harmony.

At first glance, *vástu shástra* may seem similar to *feng shui.* Both philosophies seek harmony by removing obstructions and enhancing the flow of natural energies. Both find power in five primary elements and both emphasize the importance of planetary alignment for harmonious

above *Pleasing natural illumination and convenient floor plans are hallmarks of vástu design. In keeping with ancient beliefs, the painting depicts a soothing, natural scene.*

Vástu Tips

- *Prepare a jyotish (astrological) chart.*

- *Arrange rooms according to favorable planetary alignments.*

- *Make sure doors open smoothly and swing inward.*

- *Choose nontoxic, eco-friendly fabrics and furnishings.*

- *Keep central spaces and passageways open.*

- *Set furniture and appliances slightly away from the walls.*

- *Echo two or three favorite colors through the entire house.*

- *Provide opportunities for abundant sunlight.*

- *Decorate abundantly with living foliage.*

right *A harmonious balance of fire and earth are reflected in this serene seating arrangement. Growing foliage flanks the fireplace and, in keeping with vástu teachings, the space around the chair is free of obstructions.*

placement of rooms and furnishings. However, each philosophy is deeply rooted in the culture where it was conceived and places different layers of meaning on objects and their placement.

A home designed according to *Vedic* guidelines seeks to inspire profound pleasure and inner peace by affirming the unity between all things. Rooms and furnishings that follow essential laws of nature will bring calm and fulfillment. Rooms that defy these laws are likely to provoke stress, anxiety, or depression. The rules of *vástu* are complex; however, they can be customized. Drawing upon *ayurveda*, a system of holistic health practices, the *vástu* practitioner will consider the physical and psychological elements that make up the consitution, or *dosha*, of each family member. Harmony is achieved by aligning needs of the individual with forces of nature and movement of the stars.

The *vástu* designer plays many roles, from astrologer to psychotherapist, philosopher to medical doctor. Special attention is paid to the placement of rooms and furnishings in orientation to the Sun. Harmony is expressed through a pleasing flow of colors, patterns, and textures. Abundant plant life and natural materials such as cotton, sisal, and wood affirm our connection with nature. Setting aside a special area of the home for *puja*, or worship, honors spiritual needs.

"I have ceased to question stars and books; I have begun to listen to the teaching my blood whispers to me."

Herman Hesse (1877–1962), German author

Celestial Design

Long before civilizations evolved in China and India, tribes in all parts of the world recognized the forces of the Sun, Moon, and stars. With ties close to the earth, early peoples centered their lives around seasonal planting and harvesting, cycles of the Moon, and changes in the weather. A spiritual leader, shaman, or medicine man found power and enlightenment in the wind, rain, lightning, and other forces of nature.

Many tribes honored nature's rhythms by constructing a large stone circle on a sacred site, often between intersecting rivers or on mountaintops. Perhaps the most famous of these structures is Stonehenge, a megalith monument in England. However, similar constructions have been found in every part of the world, from Egypt to Tibet to the remote Easter Island. In North and South America, some tribes created "medicine wheels"—circular arrangements of stones with radiating spokes to mark the Sun's directions or to symbolize the passage of time.

Prehistoric stone circles symbolized life as an endless cycle and also illustrated the interconnectedness of all things in the universe. The circle became a physical manifestation of natural forces and defined a spiritual space where healing and transformation could occur. During rituals and important ceremonies, the circle provided a place for tribespeople to move symbolically through stages of psychological and spiritual development. Some Native American tribes marked their stone circles with animal carvings and other symbolic objects that represented life energies.

The ancient symbols and rituals are, for the most part, lost in time. Nevertheless, we can draw much wisdom from the ancient practice of assigning energies and meanings to circular patterns and the cycles of Sun and Moon. Your house will become your own personal medicine wheel when you put special thought into where you place significant objects. Place a ceramic bird, representing spirituality and creativity, near an eastern window where it catches the first light of the rising Sun. Set aside a quiet northern corner for photo albums and leather-bound books. By honoring treasured mementos, you will begin to nourish your values, aspirations, and dreams.

🌳 serenity secret #6

Gaze at the stars. Think about how far away they are and how many years their light traveled to reach our planet. Your own problems will seem less important as you contemplate the universe.

---

opposite *African artifacts evoke a sense of timelessness in an open living space. The limited palate unifies the eclectic collection.*

Lessons from the Inca

In the remote Andes mountain range of South America, the Inca created vast stone circles according to a plan that has been handed down to their descendants. Representing natural rhythms and life energies, these stone circles, or medicine wheels, incorporated symbols and icons important in the daily life of the tribe. Carvings and other artifacts were both beautiful and powerful because they were drawn from deeply cherished ideals. Use the Inca medicine wheel as inspiration, but choose your own images to represent your most treasured values and dreams.

South: The Serpent (Sachamama). South is the direction for healing and renewal. Just as a snake slithers from its skin, we will shed the past. Although we do not forget our failures and losses, we are no longer bound by them and we are free to make new choices. The south is, therefore, an ideal location for bedrooms, bathrooms, and other places where we seek restoration.

West: The female jaguar. The west is the direction where we can best face our fears. Moving like a jaguar with grace and power, we will look death in the eye and see it not as an ending but as a transformation. In the same way, we will take inventory of our weaknesses and find quiet peace with ourselves. Kitchens, home offices, and other busy work areas are ideally placed in the west.

North: The white horse, the white buffalo, the dragon, or the hummingbird. North is where learning and wisdom occur. You will receive guidance from your ancestors and accept the collective wisdom of the human race. You may want to use the northern corner of your home for reading and study.

East: The eagle and the condor. The east is the direction of profound insight. Just as *vástu shástra* philosophies teach that we should face east when we pray and when we sleep, the Inca associated the rising Sun with spiritual awakening. With the keen vision of an eagle or a condor, we will see beyond material things and discover our true potential. Place meditation rooms or personal shrines in the eastern corner of the home.

 serenity secret #7

Make a pot out of clay. Never mind if it's lopsided. Roll up your sleeves and feel the soft, wet earth between your fingers. Shaping and reshaping the earth will help you feel more control in your life. When you are done, let your pot harden and display it as a reminder that you have the power to create the life you want for yourself and your family.

right *Prehistoric tribal customs suggest that we can achieve harmony with the universe through the careful placement of treasured objects. In this bright living area, earthen pots are arranged in orderly rows on an upper ledge. Soft, inviting chairs surround an unassuming woven bowl.*

"May serenity circle on silent wings and catch the whisper of the wind."

Cheewa James, contemporary Native American author, Modoc tribe

Answers from the Past

Exploring the belief systems of early cultures can be enlightening and transforming. Each offers its own unique perspective on how we can create environments that are in harmony with natural forces. While the philosophies differ and often contradict one another, they all teach that the objects in our daily lives are important and that the way we choose to arrange them will have an enormous impact on our physical and emotional well-being.

Choose a philosophy that reflects your cultural heritage or that resonates for you. Learn the ancient laws and follow them faithfully or simply draw on the ideas you find most useful. Don't be afraid to mingle philosophical approaches. You may choose to arrange the floor plan of your home according to a *feng shui ba-gua*, create a traditional Hindu *puja* room, and incorporate symbols drawn from Inca ideology. Or, you may do nothing more than hang a mirror to draw energy into a dingy room. Even shifting the location of a single chair will alter the atmosphere in your home. Let your instincts be a barometer: You will know that you are on the right path when you believe that change is possible.

🌳 | **serenity secret #8**

Name one fear. Write it on a scrap of paper. Place the paper in a deep, flameproof bowl and set it on fire. Envision your fear drifting away with the smoke.

---

opposite *Contemporary furnishings mingle with ancient wisdoms in this nature-loving space. Floppy, charmingly oversized leaves and a cluster of gourds celebrate life with joyful exuberance.*

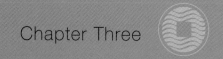

Chapter Three

Space and Movement

"We shape our buildings. Thereafter they shape us."

Winston Churchill (1874–1965), British statesman

The floor plans of our homes are the blueprints of our lives. We circle the dining table, sidestep the settee, and pace back and forth between the kitchen and family room. The way we organize our living spaces determines the amount of effort needed to complete basic household chores, affects our interaction with family members, and shapes the emotional quality of our days. ▪ Stress-free homes invite free and easy movement. Rooms and furnishings are arranged to avoid conflicts and collisions. Functionality and flexibility are key. Doors swing open smoothly, passageways are well-lit, chairs are comfortable and practical, and individual needs for space and privacy are accommodated. Rooms and furnishings are easily accessible for family members and visitors with disabilities. The home is easy to clean and maintain because clutter is eliminated and storage is conveniently located. Family disputes are avoided because busy activity centers are clearly defined and logically placed. Spaces are designed to encourage their primary functions: recreation areas invite play, office areas inspire productive work, and bedrooms enhance sleep and intimacy. ▪ Creating a more peaceful environment may mean reshaping the floor plan of your home, moving activities to different rooms, rearranging furnishings, and finding new purposes for underutilized areas. Or, you may discover that just a few minor adjustments will shift the flow of traffic in helpful ways. To determine troublespots, take a careful inventory of your entire home. Be sure to explore all the rooms, including unfinished areas such as the attic, basement, and storage areas.

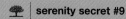 serenity secret #9

Reflect. Remember a time you felt perfectly at peace. Close your eyes and visualize your chosen place in detail. Where are you? What colors do you see? What shapes and textures? Do you hear music or other sounds? Can you sense a special aroma? Make a list of these details and begin incorporating them into your home.

opposite *A folding screen helps define a private area for quiet relaxation.*

Survey Your Space

> "A home is not a mere transient shelter: its essence lies in the personalities of the people who live in it."
>
> H. L. Mencken (1880–1956), U.S. writer and editor

opposite *A deep bathtub with a reading rack and a wall display of botanical prints transforms a tiny bathroom into a peaceful getaway.*

below *In a rustic space, festoons of white cotton gauze create a romantic, restful, and private retreat.*

Identify the areas that feel crowded and cluttered.

Observe the places where clutter accumulates: the tables that are often piled with papers and projects, the rumbled clothing tossed across chairs, the tangle of boots blocking the stairs. See the telltale fingerprints on the wall. Clues like these will reveal which parts of your home are most highly trafficked.

Sense the emotional tenor of each room.

Take a careful emotional inventory of the spaces and their furnishings. You may draw upon ancient philosophies such as *feng shui,* or listen closely to your internal sense of what feels right. Identify the areas where family and visitors gravitate and the areas that are seldom used. Look for the sore spots and the joyful places. Watch for laughter, tears, squabbles, and expressions of affection; make note where they most frequently occur.

Observe environmental conditions.

Take time to listen closely to what your dwelling is telling you. Examine the fixed structural elements: the size and shape of the room, the height of the ceiling, the size and placement of the windows, and the presence of support beams and important decorative details such as columns, mantels, and built-in shelving. Walk through each room at various times of the day and night; observe the movement of the Sun and the shifting light and shadow. Make note of sounds, aromas, and physical sensations. Check the temperature and the humidity. A warm, bright room near a bustling kitchen can be an ideal location for socializing, while a small, windowless space may be best suited for reading or meditation. A room that is too damp or chilly for most uses can often provide much-needed space for exercise equipment or laundry machines.

Honor your house.

In many ways, our dwellings tell us what they want to be. Despite our fondest wishes for an office adjacent to the kitchen or a secluded library in the basement, conditions in those spaces may make our dreams impractical. Moreover, the architectural style of the building and the topography of the surrounding landscape may suggest a personality that will become a part of the family dynamic. Imagine your home as a person. Is it male or female? Quiet or boisterous? Serious or frivolous? Allow this unique personality to find expression in the arrangement and design of its rooms.

"Always keep a place to which you can retreat."

Chinese proverb

opposite *An attic alcove flooded with sunlight is an ideal getaway for painting, writing, and other creative activities. Plenty of cross-ventilation keeps the space from becoming too warm.*

right *Bunk beds tucked into the eaves provide plenty of sleeping space for children and teens. Plush carpeting helps muffle sounds of noisy play and music.*

Know Your Needs

Each of us has a sense of territory. Sometimes these feelings are spoken: "my kitchen," "my workshop," "my desk." More frequently, we are not consciously aware of the possessiveness we feel for places and things. Acknowledging territorial needs is important because they are so often the source of tension and conflict. Sparks will certainly fly when two children feel they "own" the chair by the window. And, although two adults are not likely to come to blows over the bathroom vanity, unpleasantness will mount if they both feel they are entitled to it. As you reshape the space inside your home, you will want to make sure that each family member, including the smallest child, has a special area to call her own.

Plan for the future.

No family is immune to the forces of change. The home you plan today will be quite different from the one you'll need in the years ahead. Perhaps a flourishing business will clamor for more space, or your household may expand to include a new baby or an aging parent. Try to anticipate these changes now and your family will not be thrown into upheaval later on. Lightweight furnishings and neutral colors will permit rooms to quickly adapt to changing needs.

Make room for dreams.

Don't limit yourself to the merely pragmatic as you plan the rooms in your home. When you give an activity—or an idea—space, you acknowledge its importance and you open the way for possibilities. If you have always yearned to be a writer, set aside an area devoted to writing. Ignore the cautious and critical voices. Now is the time to design the inspiring kitchen for the aspiring gourmet cook and the attic studio for the teenager who loves to paint. By giving dreams room, you encourage them to become realities.

Create New Spaces

Ultimately, every designer must work within the boundaries of existing walls. Unless you are building a new home or doing extensive remodeling, you will need to find innovative ways to use the space you have right now. Begin with the forgotten spaces, the areas that often sit empty. Look for creative ways to utilize the attic, basement, laundry room, and garage. A damp basement may be the ideal setting for a home spa and exercise center; a heated garage could be the best spot for noisy music practice. Don't forget the small, out-of-the way nooks. The places that comfort us are often cozy and sheltered. With a lamp and a few pillows, a window alcove or a recess beneath the stairs can become a private haven.

Next, seek the rooms that are underutilized. A guestroom that is rarely visited may offer possibilities for an art studio. A dining room that sits idle can become a dynamic home theater. If children need more space for toys and play, consider giving them the master bedroom. The key is to think beyond the predictable and allow rooms to take on new, unexpected roles. As you explore possibilities, remember to look outdoors. When weather is warm, consider using the porch or deck for dining and socializing. Create a private courtyard surrounded by hedges, or turn a gazebo or pergola into an open-air living room. Sturdy and comfortable wooden furnishings and soft, colorful cushions will help assure that the outdoor area is well utilized. Playful and romantic touches such as a Persian carpet or a wingback chair will add to the illusion that your yard is an extension of your living room.

Light and color will alter the way any space is perceived, making it appear smaller or larger than it is in reality. Sunlight, natural views, and

 serenity secret #11

Let in the sunlight. Just as a plant requires light, you cannot thrive without the ultraviolet rays of natural sunshine. If the weather is overcast or you must remain indoors, spend some time in the illumination of a full-spectrum light fixture; this type of lighting is specially made to emit the frequencies needed to release mood-enhancing hormones.

"If there is room in your heart, there is room in your house."

Danish proverb

opposite *During warm weather, let the porch or patio become an extension of your living room. Lighthearted details such as a chandelier suspended from a tree branch help blur the boundaries between indoors and out.*

pastel colors—especially whites and powder blues—create the illusion of openness. To expand your space, replace bulky curtains with lightweight bamboo shades and paint walls pale, neutral tones. Install a skylight or sliding glass doors to capture life-affirming sunlight, or use bright, diffused artificial lighting to broaden the boundaries of the room. To define cozy, intimate spaces, place small lamps beside comfortable seating areas. The golden halo of incandescent bulbs will help establish a sense of privacy.

The Japanese
Nihon-ma

The traditional Japanese room, or nihon-ma, is an open and airy space that is easily reshaped according to need.

- **Fusuma:** *translucent sliding doors to partition interior spaces*

- **Shoji:** *translucent sliding doors, usually in sets of four, to separate interior from exterior spaces*

- **Ranma:** *decorative transoms for ventilation*

- **Tatami:** *rice-straw floor mats*

- **Zabuton:** *seating cushions*

- **Tokonoma:** *an alcove or corner where treasured items are placed*

- **Tokobashira:** *wooden or bamboo pillars supporting the tokonoma*

left *A contemporary cherry onda (wave) bed and a wardrobe made of translucent sliding screens capture the serene atmosphere of a traditional Japanese nihon-ma.*

above *Portable furnishings will bring new uses to for-gotten spaces. All you need is a folding chair and a lightweight table to transform a utility room or enclosed porch into a quiet retreat.*

"The art of life is a constant readjustment to our surroundings."

Kakuzo Okakaura (1862–1913), Japanese philosopher and author

Easy Movement

The term *ergonomics* is often used when describing office furnishings, but the science is a broad one that applies to every part of our built environment. It involves choosing furnishings, lighting, color, and other details that will minimize stress on our bodies and reduce the amount of effort needed to complete tasks. Consider how many steps will be needed to prepare and serve meals, supervise children, and answer phone calls. Be sure to store items close to where they will be used and avoid placing frequently used items on high shelves. Simply placing the television remote within easy reach will do much to minimize frustrations and keep peace in the family.

High-traffic areas like living rooms, television rooms, and playrooms need to be comfortable and flexible. Choose recliners rather than sofas; they are more relaxing for reading and watching television and can also be relocated more easily. In Italian, the word for furniture is *mobilia*, suggesting that tables, chairs, and other furnishings should not be fixed in place. Practical, portable furnishings open possibilities for any room, letting you alter space to meet changing needs.

Take inspiration from the traditional Japanese *nihon-ma*. Furnished entirely with cushions, mats, lightweight tables, and translucent screens, these airy spaces can be transformed at a moment's notice. You can achieve this type of fluidity simply by removing heavy, ponderous furnishings and discarding nonessentials. Tables with drop leaves and nested tables help clear floor space. Furniture on casters will easily roll to new locations. After spending time in relaxed, flexible spaces, you may notice a certain sense of buoyancy. The freedom to move the furniture can lead to other, less tangible freedoms. Rearranging the living room becomes a way to invite transformation into your life.

Universal Design

A home that minimizes stress is appealing and comfortable for people of all ages with a wide range of abilities. Even when everyone in the family is able-bodied, it is understood that some visitors may have mobility problems or visual impairments that could make parts of the home inaccessible, if not designed with sensitivity. Moreover, a sudden accident or the long-term effects of illness or aging could make mobility increasingly difficult for anyone in the household. Universal design means creating spaces that meet the needs of all people, young and old, able and disabled. Detailed guidelines are readily available from governmental housing agencies and a variety of other sources. Listed here are a few general concepts to think about as you plan your rooms.

opposite *A stress-free home enables easy movement for all people, young and old, abled and disabled. Combining beauty with functionality, this pleasant room provides several types of seating, assuring the comfort of family and visitors with differing needs.*

Designing Accessible Spaces

- *Allow enough floor space to accommodate a stationary wheelchair and also enough room for a smooth U turn: at least 198 cm (78 inches) by 152 cm (60 inches).*

- *Include tables or counters that are a variety of heights to accommodate standing, seating, and a range of different tasks.*

- *Provide shelves and a medicine cabinet that can be reached by persons seated in a wheelchair.*

- *Make sure entry doors to rooms are at least 81 cm (32 inches) wide.*

- *Mount bathroom sinks no higher than 86 cm (34 inches) from the floor.*

- *Install grab bars in the shower and beside the toilet.*

- *Provide a full-length mirror that can be viewed by all people, including children.*

- *Avoid shag carpets, uneven brick floors, and other floor surfaces that could pose slipping and tripping hazards.*

"Men cannot see their reflection in running water, but only in still water. Only that which is itself still can still the seekers of stillness."

Chuang Tzu (369?–268 B.C.), Chinese Taoist philosopher

Spiritual Spaces

For many families, serenity is rooted in a deep sense of spirituality. To foster an attitude of reverence, a special area is set aside for worship and meditation. Some Buddhist families dedicate space for a *zendo*, or meditation area. Hindu homes frequently incorporate a *puja*, or prayer room. Other faiths practice a variety of traditions, decorating their spiritual spaces with carefully chosen symbols and artifacts.

Doctors and researchers attest to the importance of following some type of spiritual activity. Meditation and prayer will not necessarily resolve problems, but taking time for quiet reflection does lower blood pressure and remove many symptoms of stress. Regardless of your faith, you may want to designate a special "serenity zone" in your home. An attic, an unfinished basement, and even a closet can become a sanctuary provided that the space is comfortable and apart from the noisy bustle of the household.

Your spirituality center need not be a place for formal religious practice, but it can help you and other members of the household pause, reconsider priorities, and rediscover the things that are truly important. Bring in artwork that represents your beliefs, fill elegant vases with fresh peonies, or set seashells on a shelf to remind you of deep oceans and rolling waves. Choosing the colors and accessories for this space can become a meaningful family activity, prompting each member of the household to clarify values and discover common bonds.

opposite *A small table with candles and a few treasured objects can become a stabilizing force in the home, providing a quiet place for prayer and meditation.*

Find Peace through Meditation

Our minds are always busy. As we go about our daily lives, we are also planning, worrying, ruminating, and anticipating. Meditation is a way to settle down the stormy seas of thought. Since ancient times, Eastern religions such as Buddhism and Hinduism have used meditation as a way to rise above worldly concerns and elevate awareness of the cosmic whole. Although traditional techniques require many years of study, you can begin meditating right now simply by focusing your attention on a single thing— an object, a mental image, a word, or your own breathing. In this way, you will help calm your busy thoughts and may quickly feel a profound sense of relaxation. If you would like to learn a formal meditation practice, you might want to begin with one of these:

🌳 | **serenity secret #12**

Seek the still place inside yourself. Inhale deeply to a count of ten, then slowly exhale, also to a count of ten. Close your eyes and listen. Imagine that your breath is the wind whirling through you, blowing away all thoughts and worries. Feel the movement deep in your abdomen, and know that you are strong.

- ***Vipassana*, or Buddhist Mindfulness Meditation**
  As you concentrate closely on an object, image, or a sound, you will observe passing thoughts and sensations without judging or analyzing. Doing this will lead you toward a calm, nonreactive Zen state of mind.

- **Transcendental Meditation (TM)**
  You will use a mantra—a repeated word or phrase—to promote deep relaxation. Any thoughts that rise to the surface of your mind are acknowledged and then gently pushed aside.

- **Visualization Meditation**
  Breathing deeply, you will visualize light or color or healing energy moving to various parts of your body. By doing this, you will ease tension, relieve pain, and promote healing.

- **Moving Meditation**
  Yoga, tai chi, and many other traditions use motion as a means toward enlightenment. Under the guidance of a master, you will learn specific postures, movements, and breathing techniques to unify mind, body, and spirit.

Chapter Four

Balance and Order

> "...No building can be said to be well designed which wants symmetry and proportion.
> In truth they are as necessary to the beauty of a building as to that of a well-formed human figure."
>
> Vitruvius (30 B.C. to A.D. 14), Roman architect

The human spirit longs for balance and order. Our own bodies are, after all, evenly proportioned with two eyes, two ears, two arms, and two legs on each side. When studied under the microscope, our cells reveal a highly ordered system of shapes and patterns, the same system found in every part of nature from swimming fish to swirling planets. Instinctively, we are calmed and reassured by environments that reflect nature's geometry. ▪ Builders of long ago knew this and sought to design spaces that were symmetrical and highly ordered. Structures like the Pyramids of Egypt, the temples of ancient Greece and Rome, the Mayan monuments, Europe's grand gothic cathedrals, and India's Taj Mahal are deeply satisfying because they express a reverence for fundamental principles of balance, order, and proportion. Although every building is a unique work of art, each echoes the archetypal forms that are the blueprints for all life. Early builders often assigned spiritual meanings to shapes and forms and to the ratios used for determining ceiling height, the placement of doors, and other architectural features. ▪ The idea that mathematical concepts have special meanings has generated a fascinating school of thought known as spiritual geometry. Some anthropologists, psychologists, and mathematicians say that certain shapes like the circle and the hexagon will influence our minds and emotions, helping us feel calm and centered. Practitioners of Eastern philosophies like *feng shui* and *vástu shástra* may combine an understanding of mathematical ratios with an awareness of energy patterns. Artists and designers frequently imbue their work with geometric symbols because they know we are shaped by the shapes around us.

opposite *This graceful chair has a slightly trapezoidal shape, suggesting strength and stability. The long, straight lines of the tall, multipaned window add to the sense of order and calm.*

You need not be mathematically gifted to draw wisdom from geometric principles. The patterns are already inside you, so you may find yourself subconsciously drawn to the most satisfying room arrangements. Play with the rhythmic repetition of designs and textures and notice how they affect the atmosphere of the room. Repeated stripes will suggest energy and excitement, while the echo of curving lines will promote a sense of calm. Look for balance and symmetry, remembering that the human form is not, itself, perfectly balanced. Try introducing an unexpected shape; don't be afraid to depart from the predictable. You will find comfort in order, but you may also find peace and joy in quirky details that express your individuality.

Lines and Shapes

If you could imagine your home without color or texture, seeing only the contours of furnishings, walls, windows, and ceilings, then you would discover a web of intersecting lines forming squares and triangles, circles and oblongs, and a variety of more complex shapes. Like Chinese calligraphy, these lines embody meanings and express emotions that may be soothing or energizing, reassuring or disturbing. They are unchanging archetypes found everywhere in the universe, from the spiral of distant galaxies to the double helix of your own genetic code.

According to Zen Buddhist beliefs, the straight line suggests supreme serenity. It is like a pond with no ripples or a single, long-sustained note. However, a perfectly straight line is not likely to occur in the natural world; it is a product of human strength and ingenuity. Straight lines may be perceived as forceful and stabilizing. Columns supporting a doorway or beams across the ceiling suggest power and quickly draw our attention. At the same time, there is a sense of tension in lines that are perfectly straight. They are like taut strings, always reminding us of forces at play. This is especially true when the lines are diagonal rather than parallel. The sharp diagonals of jutting corners can suggest conflict and discord—it's no wonder that *feng shui* advises softening angular areas with round-leafed plants.

For numerologists, shapes take on special meanings according to the numbers they suggest. The triangle, for example, is widely revered because three lines are used in its creation. Across time and cultures, the number three permeates religion and legends, from the Three Graces of ancient Greece and Rome, to the Brahma-Vishnu-Shiva of Hinduism, to the Christian holy trinity. Even more powerful is the complex hexagram form made from two triangles intertwined. With six points around a center that approximates a circle, this star formation is an ancient symbol of peace and protection and also the sacred symbol of Judaism. The interlinked triangles are often said to represent the union of opposite energies: fire and water, male and female, spirit and matter, creation and destruction, *yin* and *yang*.

When choosing room arrangements, consider the mystical powers associated with the triangle, the hexagram, and the numbers they represent. Groupings of three chairs or six photographs are inherently reassuring. Placing nine books on a shelf—instead of eight or ten—may bring an inexplicable tranquility. Numerologists would say that even the dimensions we are scarcely aware of, such as the length of tables or the height of shelves, will be more calming if they are in multiples of three. It's as though the number is encoded in our psyches, reminding us that we live in a safe and orderly universe.

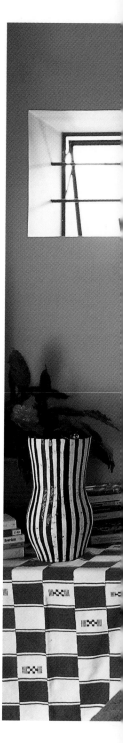

above *Repeated lines and shapes take on an almost hypnotic effect when rendered in black and white.*

"Be really whole and all things will come to you."

Lau-Tzu (604–531 B.C.), Chinese spiritual leader

Circles and Curves

Many cultures view the circle as the most perfect form. Symbolizing life's endless cycle, this is the shape of the ancient medicine wheels, the mystical *yin yang* symbol, and the timeless mandala. According to *feng shui* belief, an unbroken circle evokes high energy, *yang*, because the shape is compact. However, the Zen Buddhist *enso*, a free-form circle made with a single brushstroke, is considered more *yin*. Curved lines and relaxed *enso* shapes are inherently soothing. Our eyes tend to linger over the gentle arch of a cushioned chair or the imperfect form of hand-molded pottery. Some of the most comforting dwellings are womblike homes crafted by early peoples. Although they lacked conveniences we have grown to expect, igloos, adobe homes, and other elegantly simple shelters satisfied a deep need for soft, rounded forms.

Expressing wholeness, unity, and timelessness, circular forms are both powerful and reassuring. They reflect the Sun and Moon, the curve of the Earth, and the cycle of life and the seasons. Symbols that incorporate the circle often take on mystical significance, bringing comfort, healing, and inspiration. Incorporating circular shapes into the design of your rooms is a meaningful way to invite tranquility. Arrange furnishings into these formations, or seek these patterns in fabrics and wallcoverings. Display artwork with circle motifs, or bring inside water-smoothed stones and other samples of nature's rounded shapes.

"Imagine a hoop so large that everything is in it—all two-leggeds like us, four-leggeds, the fishes of the streams, the wings of the air, and all green things that grow. Everything is together in this great hoop."

Black Elk (1863–1950), medicine man of the Oglala Sioux Indians, as told to U.S. author John Neihardt

 serenity secret #13

Cast a circle of safety. Plant both feet firmly on the ground and feel the energy of the earth below and the sky above. Visualize this energy as warm, golden honey that will strengthen and protect you. Reach down and cup the earth energy in one hand. Reach up and gather the sky energy in your other hand. Then face your palms outward and turn a slow circle. Reach high and low to form a transparent but impenetrable sphere of energy all around you. When you sense that your safety circle is set, close your eyes and savor the feelings of comfort and security.

Soothing Circles

Mandala: In the Sanskrit language, the word *mandala* means circle, both the circumference and everything contained inside. Since ancient times, cultures around the world have used images inside a circular frame as a vehicle for spiritual transformation. Every mandala is as unique as a snowflake, expressing the inner life of the person who created it.

Yin Yang: Also known as the tai chi symbol, the ancient Chinese *yin yang* design expresses the perfect balance of opposing energies. The light and dark teardrop shapes seem to spin inside the circular frame. *Yin* is the female, passive, night energy, while *Yang* is the male, active, daylight energy. Contemplating the *yin yang* symbol is a way of affirming the harmony of the universe.

Spoked Wheel: Across time and cultures, circular shapes with radiating spokes or petals are important symbols of nature's cycles. They are found in Egyptian hieroglyphics, early Chinese ideography, Nordic folk art, and Native American icons. Contemplating the spoked wheel is a way of preparing for life's important passages.

above & opposite *Circles are the most pleasing form, according to ancient wisdoms. Use round shapes to soften corners and ease cold, linear spaces.*

🌳 **serenity secret #14**

Draw a mandala. The powerful symbol of life has brought comfort and inspiration since ancient times. Begin by drawing a circle on paper or canvas. Spontaneously draw or doodle inside the circle, creating any patterns or images that come to mind. Work without thought or plan, choosing colors or shapes as they rise to the surface of your consciousness. When your mandala is complete, you will have an evocative image of your inner self. Spend a few moments each day viewing the design and reflecting on the intricate beauty of your soul.

Triad: Three small circles nested side by side within a large circle is an almost universal symbol for unity of mind, body, and spirit. The triad, or trinity, icon is found in the art of many cultures from Tibet to ancient Europe.

Spiral: The endless swirl of an incomplete circle has symbolic meaning in many cultures, from the Celts of Great Britain to the Australian Aborigines. The design usually signifies the eternal cycle of birth, death, and rebirth.

Labyrinth: Symbolizing life's journey, the labyrinth is a meandering pathway of circles and spirals derived from the archetypal patterns of nature. When we draw a labyrinth or walk through a labyrinth garden, we travel to our own center and then return to the conscious world, enlightened and refreshed.

Enso: This empty, sweeping circle, formed by a single, relaxed brushstroke, lies at the heart of Zen Buddhist beliefs. The circumference of the circle represents the endless cycles of the material world. The emptiness in the center symbolizes the absence of mind that comes with *satori*, or the Zen state of enlightenment.

Pattern and Texture

We often think of serene places as having a smooth, uniform color. Certainly a room will not feel restful if there is an explosion of surface detailing clamoring for attention. Bold plaids, bright stripes, flashy florals, and colorful swirls create an energy that is difficult to ignore.

However, it would not be possible—or desirable—to create a room entirely devoid of pattern and texture. After all, nature itself is abundantly patterned. The delicate swirls inside a seashell, the intricate webbing of a leaf, and the exquisite speckles of color on a single stone fascinate and excite without disturbing. In the same way, you can use surface detailing to introduce depth and drama without creating discord.

Used judiciously, well-chosen prints and textures bring rhythm and movement to an otherwise uninviting room. Very small patterns create the illusion of texture, seeming almost solid from a distance. Gentle variations in colors and texture help soften kitchens, offices, and entertainment areas where appliances and machinery dominate. Simple symmetrical patterns suggest order and stability.

Because straight lines can evoke tension, striped ticking, checked gingham, and other linear patterns are best used in moderation. To soften the effect of stripes and plaids, choose muted tones and alternate patterned areas with solid blocks of color. Place the plaid pillow on an unpatterned sofa and use striped wallpaper on only one wall or on the upper or lower portion of the walls.

Patterns that feature curved flowing lines mimic forms we find in nature. Chintz fabrics with softly colored floral patterns suggest peaceful garden views. Wallpaper and stenciling with leaf-and-vine patterns help blur the boundaries between indoors and out. Special paint effects that involve sponging and stippling mimic the subtle variations we find in stone, leather, or wood. The three-dimensional character of rough plaster, brick, or stucco finishes is invitingly tactile. These natural textures take on added richness when applied with subtlety, using neutral colors.

above *Rich, earthy colors unify the patterns in a tiled kitchen wall. The curved lines of the border soften the angular diamond design.*

🌳 **serenity secret #15**

Create a Zen sand garden. For centuries, Buddhist monks have found serenity by contemplating the lines and textures of sand and stones. Although many Zen gardens are room sized, you can design one small enough to set on a tabletop. Simply fill a deep tray or baking pan with crushed granite followed by a thick layer of smooth, white sand. If you choose, you may also add a few stones or a miniature Buddha figure. Use a fork or a comb to create patterns in the sand and set aside time in your busy day to meditate on the swirling shapes and lines. When you are ready to invite change into your life, rake in new designs.

"Rhythm is our universal mother tongue. It's the language of the soul."

Gabrielle Roth, contemporary U.S. musician, philosopher, and dancer

above *Rhythm comes from the measured repetition of shapes and colors. In an all-white room, carefully placed splashes of color add excitement and also create a soothing sense of rhythm and order.*

Rhythm and Repetition

Before birth, every infant feels the steady beat of its mother's heart and, unconsciously, we all sense the rhythm of our own hearts. In design, the measured repetition of similar lines, shapes, patterns, colors, and textures creates a sense of rhythm that calms and reassures. Indeed, a room composed of disjointed, unrelated details without any sense of ordered repetition is certain to feel cluttered and chaotic.

To assure that the rhythms in your home are calming, limit yourself to a few key elements. Repeat a single color from your carpeting in a pillow, a lampshade, and a painting. Or, choose fabrics that echo variations of the wallpaper pattern. Use a single color to unify contrasting patterns and a matching pattern to unify contrasting colors. Let the rhythm come from the repetition of like things. Display collections according to color, shape and theme. Group wooden duck carvings on the mantel or hang antique tools on one wall. Also find rhythm in shapes and lines. Combine straight, linear chairs with family photographs in square frames. In a room with rounded arches, use repeated floral motifs.

While continuity is needed to establish a satisfying rhythm, too much sameness can create a room that is merely boring. Don't be afraid to introduce variation in the repeated elements. Echo several different tones from the same color family and repeat smaller or larger versions of a dominant pattern. The rhythm will be effective so long as there is a single dominant theme to unify the room.

Soothing Design

- *Soft curves*
- *Rounded forms*
- *Archetypal patterns*
- *Nature-inspired textures*
- *Repeated shapes and colors*
- *Symmetrical arrangements*
- *Balanced proportions*

Balance and Symmetry

We often use the words *centered* or *balanced* to describe how we feel when we are at peace with ourselves. The need for equilibrium is both physical and psychological: We must keep balance to walk upright and our emotions must maintain balance for us to function in our work and our relationships.

A room that is centered has a focal point or center of attention. A painting, an unusual furnishing, or an architectural feature serves as the center of attention. Balanced arrangements of shapes, colors, or patterns draw our gaze in a smooth arch around the room. Without the focal point, our attention wanders aimlessly, and without balance, we are likely to feel lopsided and insecure.

The focal point usually is not literally in the center of the space. Chances are, you would quickly tire of a perfectly symmetrical room with matching furniture arranged like mirror reflections. Instead, dissimilar objects may be balanced according to their substance, weight, or psychological powers. Two chairs beneath a window help balance a single heavy bed at the far side of the room; a grouping of sofas and chairs balances the imposing piano in the alcove; an arrangement of small photographs balances a larger portrait on the opposite wall. Balance also refers to the placement of color, pattern, and texture. A burgundy vase on the mantle balances the deep red carpet on the hearth; sheer billowy curtains balance soft cotton bed linens; floral motifs stenciled along the ceiling balance hanging pots of trailing ivy.

🌳 | **serenity secret #16**

Spend time in a rocking chair. Close your eyes and breathe with the gentle, rhythmic movement. Imagine yourself cradled in loving, protective arms. Although you are no longer an infant, you need this simple, repetitive motion to feel safe and whole.

"You must learn to be still in the midst of activity and to be vibrantly alive in repose."

Indira Gandhi (1917–1984), Indian political leader

opposite *Balanced arrangements need not be perfectly symmetrical. Here, the pillow on one chair balances the painting on the opposite wall.*

Scale and Proportion

Beauty has no size. A delicate Chippendale chair and a heavy oak banquet table have the same potential to inspire delight. Yet, we feel ill at ease the moment these two items are paired. Similarly, we may feel oppressed or overwhelmed by large, sweeping patterns in a small, confined space or a ponderous wardrobe in a tiny bedchamber. Items that are out of proportion quickly arouse anxiety and we usually don't want to be near them.

We feel the most relaxed in rooms where furnishings and details are well proportioned in relationship to each other and also to the persons who will be using them. Small children see the world from a different perspective than adults; they may feel comforted in rooms you would find claustrophobic. In contrast, a grown man is likely to feel most at ease when surrounded by objects that have heft and substance.

Contemporary homes often include expansive open spaces where family and friends gather, play games, and watch television or listen to music. The space may flow without boundaries into the dining area and kitchen, forming a single, large great room. Ultramodern loft-style homes may even place sleeping areas in the center of a vast open space.

These grand spaces impress and inspire, but they are not necessarily reassuring. Soaring cathedral ceilings can feel profoundly spiritual, or they can leave individuals feeling diminished and vulnerable. The most restful homes strike a balance between expansive open spaces and small, protected areas. To create comfort and intimacy in open areas, use color and lighting to delineate the space. By painting the walls a slightly lighter or darker tone, you establish a subtle boundary and help reduce the overwhelming size of the space. Use small table lamps with warm, incandescent bulbs to define areas with cozy pools of light. Carpets can also be very effective in establishing the sense of a room within a room.

left Plants with large, rounded leaves will release the tension of sharp, angular lines.

opposite A well-planned seating arrangement with a careful balance of shapes, lines, colors, and textures will set the scene for peaceful meals. In some traditions, the number three is considered sacred.

opposite Unexpected combinations of colors and textures entice the sense of touch. Here, timeworn stones against the grain of natural oak create a soothing counterpoint to cool metallic chairs.

Unity and Harmony

Carefully composed, harmonious rooms are deeply relaxing. We feel centered because objects are arranged with sensitivity for scale, proportion, and balance. The thoughtful placement of shapes and the measured repetition of colors and patterns help unify the space, creating a "look" or ambiance.

You need not limit yourself to matching furniture or coordinated patterns to create harmony. Strong color accents echoed in fabric designs and artwork can unify even the most startling combinations. A consistent use of shapes, patterns, or textures will also bind together elements that, on first glance, do not appear to match.

Dare to place a primitive wood carving on a mahogany sideboard. Try mingling crystal with clay, chrome with oak, silk with sisal. Unexpected partnerships will work as long as there is a connecting theme. The tie that binds can be a specific style such as French Country or Art Moderne, but more frequently the sense of unity will come from the personalities of the people using the space. Choose furnishings and objects you truly love and you may be surprised at how well they harmonize. Incorporate details that express the differing—and even conflicting—tastes and interests of your family. Finding harmony and order in the midst of differences is a potent way to reinforce family stability.

"All that is harmony for thee, O Universe, is in harmony with me as well."

Marcus Aurelius (A.D. 121–180), Roman emperor

Chapter Five

Color and Light

"Colors . . . follow the changes of the emotions."

Pablo Picasso (1881–1973), Spanish artist

One of the most important things you can do to reduce the level of stress in your home is to choose calming colors that speak to your spirit. From creamy neutral tones to deep indigo, colors act as subtle yet powerful drugs, affecting both body and mind. ▪ In ancient times, physicians in China, India, and Egypt practiced *chromotherapy,* the science of stimulating physical and mental energies through color. Today, some therapists use colored lights to treat a wide range of ailments. Designers now pay close attention to the impact of color when they create interiors for hospitals, schools, stores, and restaurants. ▪ Indeed, color is so powerful that its influence is felt even when we are sleeping. Everyone, including those without sight, senses color because it is actually composed of vibrating light waves. Perceived through the skin as well as the eyes, these waves stir physiological responses that are instinctive and universal. Warm tones like yellow, orange, and red act as stimulants. They increase our pulse and respiration and may produce either excitement or anxiety. Cool colors such as blue and green are calming. They decrease our pulse and respiration and may encourage relaxation.

 serenity secret #18

Contemplate a color. Visualize a shade that represents qualities you need in your life today. Close your eyes and breathe deeply. Imagine your chosen color filling your lungs and feel it flowing into your arms and legs. Hold the color inside and accept its power to comfort and heal. Exhale slowly, letting the color swirl around your head. Then, once again, breathe deeply, inhaling your chosen color.

opposite *Blue, yellow, and green are a playful but harmonious mix in an informal dining area. The napkins, china, and flowers echo the cheerful scheme and help balance the colors.*

above *Splashes of yellow introduce a spirit of joy and playfulness in a snow-white room. Carried through the house, the yellow details harmonize rooms and convey a sense of family unity.*

"Simplicity is the ultimate sophistication."

Leonardo da Vinci (1452–1519), Italian Renaissance artist and scientist

opposite *A balanced arrangement of matching chairs creates a sense of calm and order. Fitting perfectly in the angular alcove, the square table holds a single, simple centerpiece.*

In Times of Excess Responsibility . . .

Ringing telephones. Crying babies. Bills to pay, papers to write, meals to prepare, and meetings to attend. Often it seems that there is no relief from the frantic pace of an ordinary day. The things that have deep, lasting value—family, creative pursuits, spirituality—are pushed aside in the hubbub of frantic activity. Meals are skipped, sleep is lost, and, without proper nutrition and rest, it becomes increasingly difficult to meet deadlines and make clear decisions.

When life becomes too busy and too complicated, it is time to simplify your home décor. Clear away the clutter that rattles at your nerves; embrace minimalist design. Choose uncomplicated patterns and neutral colors: cream, pearl gray, and dusty pastels. Use simple shapes and straight lines to create a sense of order and direction. Remove bulky fabric window treatments and set fruit in an orderly arrangement on the kitchen counter. Seek symmetry. Place a single small table between matching chairs. Remove furnishings that are rarely used and collections that merely gather dust. You will begin to feel a sense of freedom simply by creating clean, open spaces.

■ **Where to Begin**
Seek Simplicity

When you are feeling exhausted and overwhelmed by responsibilities and obligations:

- Clear obstacles from passageways.
- Minimize collections and decorative details.
- Combine light, neutral colors with the golden tones of natural wood.
- Remove light-obscuring window treatments; fill rooms with soul-warming sunlight.
- Replace wall-to-wall carpeting with natural pine, oak, maple, or ash.
- Choose lightweight, functional tables, shelves, and seating.
- Emphasize confident, straight lines.
- Seek symmetrical, balanced arrangements.
- Add the calming fragrance of cedar or marjoram.
- Ensure that all doors and windows open easily, even if you never use them.

In Times of Insecurity
and Worry . . .

May you live in interesting times is the ancient saying that has become the double-edged sword of the modern world. Information technology has created a global village, expanding our awareness and also our fears. Satellites spin around the Earth, transmitting waves of digital information about desert armies. World events seem beyond our control, yet they impact our lives. Stability that we once knew, or thought we knew, seems elusive. We may discover that we can no longer count on the security of a job, the refuge of a relationship, the solidity of our health, the permanence of our money supply, or the seemingly good intentions of the person next-door.

When the stress of interesting times disrupts the harmony of your home, seek comfort in art, treasured heirlooms, and objects that bring you joy. Instead of an austere, minimalist environment, you may need paintings on the wall, a cluster of smooth onyx carvings, and favorite books stacked beside a molded chair. Incorporate circular forms and soft, rounded shapes. Let in sunlight, but provide translucent blinds to filter out the afternoon glare. Soften floors with textured woolen rugs. Find comfort in the repeated colors and patterns of floral prints or decorative stenciling. Most importantly, indulge yourself with a crystal vase of fragrant roses or gardenias and listen closely to nature's healing music.

■ Where to Begin
Find Comfort

During times of worry and insecurity:

- Seek soothing *yin* energy: choose flowing lines and soft, graceful forms.
- Fill elegant crystal vases with blooming roses and other fragrant flowers.
- Create cozy, comforting nooks with soft cushions and reassuring sunlight.
- Combine warm amber hues with deeply soothing shades of pink and rose.
- Provide soft, diffused lighting.
- Cover floors with colorful woven rugs.
- Develop a motif of repeated patterns and colors.
- Display family photographs, paintings, and treasured artifacts.
- Store newspapers and newsmagazines out of sight.
- Remove televisions from bedrooms, kitchens, and dining areas.

 serenity secret #45

Laugh. Exchange jokes with friends or watch a comedy on television. The humor will lift your spirits and the laughter will actually change your body chemistry. Your level of stress hormones—cortisol and adrenaline—will decrease, and you'll feel less bothered by irritations and better able to handle frustrations.

"A man's fortune must first be changed from within."

Chinese proverb

opposite *The city beyond this high-rise window is a constant reminder of worldly pressures and anxieties. Inside, however, rounded shapes and soft, golden hues create a soothing atmosphere. The pink rose blossoms are echoed on the painted chair.*

"Enjoy to the full the resources that are within thy reach."

Pindar (c. 518–438 B.C.),
Greek lyrical poet

left *Fresh flowers, an elegant vase, and a row of crystal bottles bring luxury to this pleasant bathing area. An expansive wall mirror captures the sunlight and reflects peaceful views.*

opposite *Gold, copper, and bronze suggest luxury, yet they are earthy and sensual. To create an aura of comfort and ease, define your space with a folding screen painted in luminescent metallics.*

In Times of Frustration . . .

All too often, what disrupts our inner peace is not the weighty world events but life's petty annoyances. The ringing of a cell phone or booming music from the house next door intrude into our private space. A missing paycheck, a tardy employee, a traffic jam, and countless other delays and inconveniences try our patience. A broken light switch, a baffling computer program, or an uncooperative teenager can push us to the edge.

To ease the stress of life's petty annoyances and frustrations, concentrate on redirecting the flow of energy—*chi*—through your home. Sense the emotional tenor of each room and of each occupant. Insulate your home against noise and distractions, repair or dispose of broken appliances, and develop a system for keeping pesky piles of papers from collecting on the kitchen table. Then, to ease your nerves and calm your spirit, seek ways to indulge yourself and your family. Suggest abundance with warm, metallic colors: copper, bronze, brass, and gold. Focus on sensual details. Introduce textures that entice the sense of touch and fill rooms with the soothing fragrances of sage and sandlewood. Turn your bathroom into a center for hydrotherapy and your bedroom a haven for love.

■ **Where to Begin**

Nourish the Senses

When petty annoyances rattle at your serenity:

- Combine lush metallic colors with uncomplicated lines and shapes.
- Seek the cool sensuality of smooth marble, glass, steel, and brass.
- Use oversized mirrors to capture pleasing views.
- Place seating areas where they will receive the most sunlight.
- Emphasize luxury in bathing areas; provide plenty of plush towels and scented soaps.
- Design for sensuality in the bedroom; set fragrant candles on the bureau and hang a light-capturing crystal in the window.
- Repair leaky faucets, squeaky doors, and other sources of irritation.
- Replace flickering fluorescent lights with soothing incandescent fixtures.
- Turn off computers and other electronic equipment when not in use.
- Mask outside noise with recordings of falling rain, or make your own music through singing, chanting, or drumming.

In Times of Conflict . . .

Wherever two or more people live together under a single roof, conflicts will occur. Lifemates may disagree over anything from finances to fidelity, while children learning to express their independence will inevitably quarrel with their parents. Within the extended family called a nation, religion and politics are continual sources of discord. Moreover, internal conflicts—indecision and mixed emotions—are a common source of stress for every thinking person.

When you find your stress mounting because of family disagreements, it is time to seek harmony in home design. Look for ways to unify rooms with color, pattern, and texture. Spiraling lines and curving forms will help draw together different elements in a room. Choose artwork that echoes the structural shapes of windows, doors, and stairways. Maintain a consistent color scheme through the entire home. Suggest harmony by arranging objects in paired groupings. Seemingly small details can go a long way in easing family conflicts. Simply placing matching chairs side by side may help soothe a troubled marriage.

■ Where to Begin
Encourage Harmony

When conflict and discord upset family life:

- Arrange rooms and furnishings to avoid conflicts and collisions; keep central spaces and passageways open.
- Select a family color and incorporate it into the scheme for each room.
- Use area rugs and soft, flowing drapery.
- Set furniture and appliances slightly away from the walls.
- Emphasize circular, oval, and spiral forms.
- Place a symbol of welcome in the front entryway.
- Incorporate details drawn from several cultures.
- Display objects in paired groupings.
- Provide subdued lighting; avoid harsh, bright lights.
- Create inviting communal spaces to invite dialog.

 serenity secret #47

Talk. Find someone who listens well—a friend, a family member, a spiritual leader, or a counselor—and express your feelings openly. As you verbalize your fears, they will have less power over you. Moreover, connecting with another human being will comfort and strengthen you.

"Nothing can bring you peace but yourself."

Ralph Waldo Emerson (1803–1882),
U.S. poet and essayist

opposite *Suggesting the archetypal symbol for life's eternal cycle, twisting spiral forms are expressed in this staircase and echoed in the framed artwork. In many traditions, a set of two matching chairs represents marital harmony.*

In Times of Loss . . .

Surely there is no stress so devastating as loss. The end of a relationship, divorce, unemployment, failing health, sudden disability—many events can shake us from the lives we used to call "normal." Perhaps the greatest loss that one can bear is the death of a beloved partner, a child, or a friend. Even the loss of a pet can turn our world upside down.

When you are grieving, it is especially important to make sure that your home feels nurturing and life affirming. Find comfort in solid, earthen things; surround yourself with unpainted wood, rough-hewn stone, and deep red brick. Decorate abundantly with living plants in handcrafted pottery. A ceiling-high ficus tree and hanging pots of Boston fern will bring their own quiet energy into your space. Also, don't forget the healing power of animal companions. While you may not feel ready to take on the responsibility of a dog or cat, now is a good time to start an aquarium or place a bird feeder outside your window.

 serenity secret #48

Give yourself permission to cry. Shedding tears is nature's way of cleansing your body of chemicals that accumulate in your body during times of stress. Researchers have also found that crying helps lower the blood pressure and pulse rate. Tears cannot remove your sorrow, but they will help you grow strong enough to cope and to move forward with your life.

■ Where to Begin
Evoke Nature

During times of loss:

- Surround yourself with wood, stone, clay, and other reminders of nature.
- Use warm, earthy colors—browns, greens, golds, and deep russet.
- Decorate abundantly with living plants.
- Choose fabrics and materials that tantalize the sense of touch; mingle rugged stone with soft velvet, cool marble with shimmering silk.
- Gradually remove items that evoke painful memories; move at your own pace.
- Design with water: Create a tabletop fountain or an indoor pond.
- Start an aquarium or place a bird feeder outside your window.
- Install full-spectrum light fixtures in darker rooms.
- Seek eco-friendly materials that are biodegradable and recyclable.
- Create a home sanctuary for meditation and reflection.

opposite Brick, wood, and rich, earthy colors combine in this comforting seating area. On the sofa, velvet pillows and an embroidered throw add an enticing touch of luxury and warmth.

"The soul would have no rainbow had the eyes no tears."

John Vance Cheney (1895–1919), U.S. poet

"Preserve the old, but know the new."

Chinese proverb

above *Meaningful objects are more than merely decorative. In this sunny bedroom, animal sculptures are carefully placed to inspire dreams and to symbolically evoke their own special energies. The bed with its vivid fuchsia covers radiates an aura of tropical adventure and celebrates the possibility for new beginnings.*

above *Harmony is expressed in a simple grouping of three small urns. Although their colors and patterns are quite different, the urns are unified by their similar shapes. Two tidy storage boxes stacked beneath the table suggest a readiness to move on.*

In Times of New Beginnings . . .

As predictable as the ebb and flow of the tides, cycles of change are part of our everyday lives. Growth from childhood to adolescence to middle age seems to happen all too quickly. Whether changes are anticipated or come to us by surprise, life's transitions can leave us feeling unsettled and disoriented. New marriages, new homes, new neighborhoods, new jobs, new babies, new relationships may be cause for celebration, yet they will also arouse fear and anxiety.

Decorative details that symbolize strength will help you feel more secure during times of transition. Take this opportunity to experiment with exciting new colors, patterns, and details. Choose furnishings and arrangements that can be quickly adapted. Discard nonessentials, but display artifacts passed down from your grandparents or artwork that reflects your cultural heritage. These will help ground you in time and space as you move forward. Appreciate transition as a part of life's adventure. Consider holding a family ceremony to commemorate life's passages: light candles, burn incense, and sing, chant, or play musical instruments.

■ **Where to Begin**

Embrace Change

During times of transition:

- Remove bulky carpeting and draperies.
- Choose lightweight tropical woods.
- Arrange furnishings for easy accessibility.
- Suggest a spirit of adventure with bright, daring colors.
- Bring in exotic orchids or tropical bird-of-paradise flowers.
- Include artwork that will remind you of your heritage or family history.
- Add wicker, cane, and straw accents.
- Hang wind chimes in the windows.
- Burn incense and naturally scented candles.
- Keep in mind the power of numbers: Cluster decorative items in groups of three, six, or nine.

🌳 | **serenity secret #49**

Make lists. Write down the things you must do today and put the most urgent tasks at the top. Also record long-range goals: where you hope to be next month, next year, and five years from today. Even if you don't achieve everything you'd like, you'll feel more in control. Plus, you'll feel a satisfying sense of accomplishment each time you cross an item off your list.

Create a Serenity Zone

A home that soothes and heals is not created overnight. You may find yourself making many changes before one small shift—a bright pillow tossed onto the sofa, a vase of branches beside a window, a brighter bulb in the hallway lamp—creates an entirely new atmosphere. Perhaps you will sense a wave of serenity the moment you step across your threshold. Or, awareness may dawn gradually as you awaken to soul-warming sunlight, feeling unusually calm and deeply rested.

In mystical and spiritual thought, the ideal is to move beyond worldly worries to a transcendent state, a sense of oneness with the universe. Zen Buddhists know it as *satori,* spiritual leaders from India describe *advaita,* while Quakers speak of sensing the *inner light*. On a more pragmatic level, creative artists often refer to a magical state of mind when ideas and inspiration seem to flow from pen or brush. Musicians sometimes speak of being in another dimension when they are truly in tune with the music, playing notes that are not merely correct but in synch with something otherworldly. Athletes use the phrase "in the zone" to describe the magical place where the golfer has a perfect swing, the basketball player scores on every shot, and the baseball player knows instinctively what pitch is coming and wills the bat to strike dead center.

Designing spaces in our homes is a way of reaching for a type of zone where we can feel safe and protected, loved and loving, creative and productive, and completely at peace. *Feng shui, vástu shástra,* prehistoric rituals, color therapy, aromatherapy, and various other design techniques are all tools to help move us toward that ideal. They become most effective when we use them with an understanding of what our homes mean to us and what changes we need to invite into our lives.

Some psychologists believe that we all have the power to tap into the spiritual realm known as the superconscious. It is quite possible that redesigning our interiors can help us attain a new vision of the ordinary, where simple joys lead to deeper insights, the familiar becomes the inspired, and windows open onto a more peaceful way of life.

Serene Spaces Provide . . .

- *Physical safety*
- *Emotional security*
- *Privacy*
- *Comfort*
- *Flexibility and adaptability*
- *Sensual pleasures*
- *Connection with nature*
- *Creativity and self-expression*
- *A sense of heritage*
- *Hope for the future*
- *Spiritual renewal*

 serenity secret #50

Open a window. Move a table. Add a beautiful detail that speaks to your soul. Creating a joyful and serene life begins with simple actions. Make just one small change, starting today.

"May the warm winds of Heaven
    blow softly on your home,
And the Great Spirit bless all
    who enter there.
May your moccasins make happy tracks
    in many snows,
And may the rainbow always touch
    your shoulder."

Cherokee blessing

above *A vase of branches echoes the trees outside and helps direct the flow of energies through this serene, open space. Abundant sunlight and natural views assure a restful atmosphere.*

BUYER'S GUIDE:
Resources for Creating a Stress~Free Home

Many elements go into creating a serene, stress-free home. The suppliers listed here offer a
wide range of products, from decorative accents to fragrances and relaxation tools. Most have
worldwide distribution centers or international mail order via the Internet.

ancient wisdoms

Ananda Assisi Coop. a r.l.
Casella Postale 48
06088 Santa Maria degli Angeli (PG)
Italy
075-9148505
(fax) 075-9148506
www.innerlife.it
*Products, including Sri Yantras, that enhance
the inner spiritual life*

Ayurveda Holistic Center
www.ayurvedahc.com
*Ayurvedic books, dosha kits, and copper
Vedic yantras*

FastFengShui
415 Dairy Road #E-144
Kahului, HI 96732 USA
808-891-8488
(fax) 808-891-0065
www.fastfengshui.com
*Feng shui–inspired products,
aromatherapy to water fountains, including
Clutter Clearers*

So Inspired
20 St. Christophers Court
102 Junction Road
London N19 5QT
UK
(tel./fax) 020-7263-2727
www.soinspired.com
*Gifts of the spirit—aromatherapy, feng shui,
chakra balancing, and crystals*

Vedic Resource
P.O. Box 926337
Houston, TX 77292 USA
713-290-8715; 1-800-829-2579
(fax) 713-290-8720
www.vedicresource.com
*Beads, music, yantras, Vastu workbooks, and
Vedic charts*

decorative accents

Bhargava and Co.
435/A-1, Shak & Nahar Industrial Estate
Lower Parel, Bombay
400 013, Maharashtra
India
91-22-493-0950
(fax) 91-22-493-0949
www.indianmusicals.com
Musical instruments from India

KISEIDO
2255 29th Street, Suite 4
Santa Monica, CA 90405 USA
800-988-6463
(fax) 310-578-7381
www.kiseido.com
*Offers elegant, decorative gameboards for
Go, the ancient Yin and Yang game.*

The Longaberger Company
One Market Square
1500 East Main Street
Newark, OH 43055 USA
740-322-5900
www.longaberger.com
Handcrafted basketry

Marimekko Oyi
Puusepänkatu 4
00880 Helsinki, Finland
358-9-75871
www.marimekko.fi
*To the trade only; clothing, interior decoration,
and accessories*

Mid-East Mfg.
P.O. Box 1523
Emanabad Road
Sialkot
Pakistan
92 (432) 542029
(fax) 92 (432) 551679
www.mid-east.com.pk
*Manufacturers of ancient drums and other
instruments*

Mejiro Co., Ltd.
3-17-30 Shimo Ochiai, Shinjuku-ku
Tokyo 161 0033
Japan
81-(0)3-3950-0051
(fax) 81-(0)3-3950-5492
www.mejiro-jp.com
www.mejiro-jp.com/eng/e_home.html (English)
*Crafters of traditional Shinobue and
Shakuhachi, Japanese bamboo flutes*

Mauviel
B.P. 28
Route de Caen
50800 Villedieu-les-Poêles
France
33 (0) 2 33 61 00 31
(fax) 33 (0) 2 33 50 74 55
www.mauviel.com
Beautiful and functional cooking products

Raja Inc.
3167 San Mateo NE #210
Albuquerque, NM 87110 USA
505-880-0257
(fax) 505-880-0258
www.rajainc2.com
*Handmade rugs, baskets, and decor from
southwestern USA*

Red Eagle Gallery
1034 SW Taylor Street
Portland, OR 97205 USA
503-827-8551
(fax) 503-827-8597
www.redeaglegallery.com
Sculpture, batiks, and baskets from Zimbabwe

Ruffoni
Via Magenta, 5
P.O. Box 11
28887 Omegna VB
Italy
39-0323-61990
(fax) 39-0323-866109
www.ruffonionline.com
*Classic Italian copper products for the kitchen
and home*

Salamó
Padró, 54
17100 La Bisbal d Empord
(GIRONA)
Spain
(tel./fax) 972640255
www.salamoceramica.com
Manufacturer of traditional pottery for
domestic use since the eighteenth century

Sambuco Mario & C. snc
Via della Tecnica
06053 Deruta (PG) I
Italy
39 075 9711625
(fax) 39 075 9711750
www.sambuco.it
Artistic ceramics, majolica, and
terra-cotta pottery

Serenity Health
PMB 49
P.O. Box 7530
Yelm, WA 98597 USA
888-890-5764
(fax) 360-894-0785
www.serenityhealth.com
Handcrafted indoor water fountains, tabletop
fountains, and waterfalls

Spiegel
800-527-1577
www.spiegel.com
Accent tables and chairs, storage, and
decorative items

WANDOO Didgeridoo
38 Curedale Street
Beaconsfield WA 6162
Australia
(08) 9336 2128
www.wadidge.com.au
Authentic Australian didgeridoos, ancient
Aboriginal instruments

Zimmer + Rohde
Zimmersmühlenweg 14-16
61440 Oberursel/Frankfurt
Germany
49 6171 632 02
www.zimmer-rohde.com
To the trade only; silks, transparent fabrics,
and pile weaves

bath and spa

Belhydro
Zwaaikomstraat 72
8800 Roeselare, Belgium
32 (0)51 24 05 08
(fax) 32 (0)51 24 62 80
www.belhydro.be
Whirlpools, bathtubs, steam enclosures, saunas

Kohler
444 Highland Drive
Kohler, WI 53044 USA
800-456-4537
www.kohler.com
Deep soaking tubs and other luxury fixtures

Sanijet
1461 S. Beltline Road, Suite 100
Coppell, TX 75019 USA
972-745-2283
(fax) 972-745-2285
www.sanijet.com
Manufactures pipeless whirlpool tubs

Showerlux U.K. Limited
Sibree Road
Coventry, West Midlands CV3 4FD
UK
(44) (024) 76-639400
(fax) (44) (024) 76-305457
www.duscholux.com
Product line includes combined steam and
shower room

floor coverings

Advance Flooring Company
131 Captain Springs Road Onehunga
P.O. Box 13184
Auckland
New Zealand
09-634-4455 or 0508-238-262
www.ralenti.co.nz/advance
Natural flooring products, including sisal, coir,
seagrass, and leather

The Alternative Flooring Company, Ltd.
Unit 3b Stephenson Close
East Portway Industrial Estate
Andover, Hampshire, SP10 3RU
UK
01264 335111
(fax) 01264 336445
www.alternative-flooring.co.uk
Natural fiber flooring products, including jute,
sisal, wool, seagrass, and coir

Eco-Friendly Flooring
100 S. Baldwin Street, Suite 110
Madison, WI 53703 USA
608-698-0571; 866-250-3273
(fax) 608-834-9000
www.ecofriendlyflooring.com
Wholesale supplier of cork, bamboo, sisal,
and hemp flooring, recycled glass tile, nontoxic
decking, and granite countertops

Sisal Rugs Direct
888-613-1335
www.sisalrugs.com
Custom maker of natural fiber area rugs
in the USA

furnishings and storage

California Closets
www.calclosets.com
Customized storage solutions; worldwide
distribution

Carolina Morning Designs
5790 Highway 80 South
Burnsville, NC 28714 USA
888-267-5366
www.zafu.net
Designs and manufactures traditional
meditation furniture

Harmony In Design
2050 S. Dayton Street
Denver, CO 80231 USA
303-337-7728
(fax) 303-337-8247
www.harmonyindesign.com
Yoga, meditation, and ergonomic furniture

IKEA
www.ikea.com
Simple ergonomic furniture designs; worldwide
distribution

Laura Ashley Ltd
27 Bagleys Lane
Fulham, SW6 2QA
UK
0870 562 2116
www.lauraashley.com
Occasional furniture, wardrobes, bedding,
and curtains

Maine Cottage Furniture
207-846-1430
(fax) 207-846-0602
www.mainecottage.com
Flexible painted wood furnishings

Roche-Bobois
www.roche-bobois.com
Practical furnishings that reflect a blend of
periods and styles

R.O.O.M.
Alstromergaten 20, Box 49024
SE-100 28 Stockholm
Sweden
(46) 8-692-5000
(fax) (46) 8-692-5060
www.room.se
Flexible, functional furnishings, storage,
and decorative accents

Sentient
244 Fifth Avenue, Suite 2117
New York, NY 10010 USA
(tel./fax) 212-772-0112
www.meditationchair.com
Meditation chairs and other ergonomic
furnishings

fragrance, incense, and essential oils

Audrey Leigh Essential Oils
The Old Creamery, Gelli Lane,
Nannerch CH7 5QR
UK
(44) 01352-741-511
(fax) (44) 01352-741-838
www.audreyleigh.com
Therapeutic-quality essential oils

Baieido Co., Ltd.
1-1-4 Kurumano-cho Higashi, Sakai City,
Osaka 590-0943,
Japan
072-229-4545
(fax) 072-227-1672
www.baieido.co.jp/english
Baieido Japanese incense

BIOSUN GmbH
35641 Schwalbach
P.O. Box 100
Germany
49 64 45 / 60 07-0
(fax) 49 64 45 / 60 07-600
www.biosun.de
Hopi and essential-oil ear candles, relaxation CDs, and lotions

The Essential Oil Company
1719 SE Umatilla Street
Portland, OR 97202 USA
800-729-5912
In Oregon: 503-872-8772
(fax) 503-872-8767
www.essentialoil.com
Unscented lotions that may be combined with various essential oils

The Essential Oil Company Ltd
Worting House
Church Lane, Basingstoke
Hampshire RG23 8PX
UK
01256 332 737
(fax) 01256 332 119
www.eoco.org.uk/
Essential oils, burners, books, magnotherapy products, and aromatherapy accessories

New Directions Aromatics
21-B Regan Road
Brampton, Ontario L7A 1C5
Canada
905-840-5459; 877-255-7692
(fax) 905-846-1784
www.poyanaturals.com/
Wildcrafted essential oils

Nutraceutic, Inc.
P.O. Box 358331
Gainesville, FL 32635-8331 USA
888-543-9294; 352-371-3735
(fax) 815-301-8667
www.thenagchampacompany.com
Online broker of Satya Sai Baba Nag Champa Indian soaps, incense, and aromatherapy products

lighting

Duro-Test Lighting
12401 McNulty Road, Suite 101
Philadelphia, PA 19154 USA
800-289-3876
(fax) 888-959-7250
www.durotest.com
Designer of Vita-Lite, a fluorescent lamp that simulates natural daylight

Environmental Lighting Concepts
P.O. Box 172425
Tampa, FL 33672-0425 USA
813-621-0058; 800-842-8848
(fax) 813-626-8790
www.ott-lite.com
Developers of OTT-LITE products, made from a blend of earth phosphors

Full Spectrum Solutions
4880 Brooklyn Road
Jackson, MI 49201 USA
888-574-7014
(fax) 517-764-4029
www.fullspectrumsolutions.com
www.paralite.com
Makers of ParaLite and UltraLux brand full-spectrum lamps with low mercury

OneTech, L.L.C.
23 Acorn Street
Providence, RI 02903 USA
401-273-5316; 877-663-8324; 514-984-6340
(fax) 401-273-0630
www.onetech.net
Developer of the Eclipse Computer light, which helps reduce eyestrain and computer vision syndrome (CVS)

Verilux
9 Viaduct Road
Stamford, CT 06907 USA
203-921-2430; 800-786-6850
(fax) 203-921-2427
www.verilux.net
Lighting products that simulate the full spectrum of natural light

relaxation tools

Amida
P.O. Box 1058
Nevada City, CA 95959 USA
800-292-4057
(fax) 530-265-4704
www.ami-da.com
Online store for meditation supplies, yoga products, and ceremonial teas

Arcturus Star Products
25401 County Road F
Cortez, CO 81321 USA
970-564-5811; 888-730-1053
(fax) 970-564-5812
www.arcturusstar.com
Products that balance the human bioenergy system by harmonious vibrations

Askland Technologies, Inc
P.O. Box 2620
Victorville, CA 92393 USA
800-542-7782; 760-949-7678
(fax) 760-949-7868
www.zen-clocks.com
Zen clocks with a gentle, progressive alarm function

BioWaves, LLC.
14150 NE 20th Street, Suite 121
Bellevue, WA 98007 USA
425-895-0050; 800-734-3588
www.biowaves.com
Designer of tools for vocal analysis and low-frequency sound therapy

Brighten Color Flame Candles, Inc.
5125 Convoy Street, Suite 201
San Diego, CA 92111 USA
858-277-2263
www.brightencolorflame.com
Designer, manufacturer, and retailer of colored-flame lamp oils and candles

The Center for Neuroacoustic Research
701 Garden View Court
Encinitas, CA 92024 USA
760-942-6749
(fax) 760-942-6768
www.neuroacoustic.com
Scientific sound-therapy products, including the Ergonomic Zero-Gravity Acoustic Vibration Recliner, sound-therapy tables, goggles, and CDs

Gaiam Relaxation Company
360 Interlocken Boulevard, Suite 300
Broomfield, CO 80021 USA
303-222-3600
(fax) 303-222-3700
www.therelaxationcompany.com
Musical and spoken-word relaxation and meditation programs

HoMedics, Inc.
3000 Pontiac Trail, Department 168
Commerce Township, MI 48390 USA
800-HOMEDICS (800-466-3342)
www.homedics.com/
Massagers, aromatherapy, sound therapy, and
other personal-wellness products

Pacific Light
2212 Queen Anne Avenue N #322
Seattle, WA 98109 USA
877-835-0838
www.healing-peace.com
Audio and videotapes for relaxation,
meditation, and healing

Sound Therapy International
P.O. Box A2237
Sydney South NSW 1235
Australia
61-2-9665-1777
(fax) 61-2-9664-9777
www.soundtherapyinternational.com
Self-help sound-therapy program

TenRen
380 Swift Avenue, Suite 5
South San Francisco, CA 94080 USA
650-583-1044
www.tenren.com
Chinese tea products

Theta Technologies
877-4FASHION
www.hypnopage.com
Light and sound machines for adjusting
mental focus

Photographers

Courtesy of Laura Ashley
Ltd./www.laurashley.com, 39; 68; 78; 117;
   118; 151

Todd Caverly, Brian Vanden Brink Photos/Luigi
Bartolomeo, Architect, 51

Guillaume DeLaubier, 7; 8; 47; 55; 147

Carlos Domenech/Michael Wolk, Design, 43;
   155

Tria Giovan, 25; 29; 30; 84; 88; 99; 112; 121;
   122

Reto Guntli, 35; 45; 49; 56; 125; 127; 141

John Edward Linden/Fernau & Hartman
Architects, 37

Courtesy of Maine Cottage
Furniture/www.mainecottage.com, 11; 20; 24;
   58; 65; 95

Courtesy of Roche-Bobois/www.roche-
bobois.com, 26; 40; 60; 91; 101; 102; 133; 152

Courtesy of R.O.O.M./www.room.se, 62; 74; 85;
   98; 113; 130; 131; 138

Eric Roth, 4; 14; 17; 19; 34; 36; 66; 72;
   75 (bottom); 76; 77; 79; 83; 93; 96; 100;
   139

Tim Street-Porter/www.beateworks.com,
   81; 87; 114; 124

Brian Vanden Brink, 22; 23; 129; 135; 136; 137;
   142; 145; 149

Brian Vanden Brink/Stephen Blatt, Architect, 71

Brian Vanden Brink/Axel Berg, Builder &
Morningstar Marble & Granite, 146

Brian Vanden Brink/Design Group Three,
Architect & Christina Oliver Interior Design, 107

Brian Vanden Brink/Dominic Merca Dante,
Architect, 104

Brian Vanden Brink/Elliott & Elliott Architects,
   41

Brian Vanden Brink/Christina Oliver Interior
Design, 153

Brian Vanden Brink/Quinn Evans, Architect, 111

Brian Vanden Brink Photos/Winton Scott
Architect, 61

Courtesy of Zimmer + Rohde,
Textile manufacturers of three different lines:
Ardecora, Etamine and Zimmer + Rohde, 3; 12;
   52; 53; 70; 75 (top)

About the Author

Jackie Craven is a widely published writer who specializes in architecture and interior design. She is the author of *The Healthy Home,* from Rockport Publishers, a columnist for *House & Garden* magazine, and a correspondent for the architecture pages at About.com. Passionate about historic buildings, Jackie finds peace and joy in restoring Victorian houses on her street in upstate New York. Visit her online at www.jackiecraven.com.